In **Divine Favor** author Bou
the pastoral ministry that is
stabbing and malicious gossi
expect it, not excluding those in the household of faith. He frames
his experiences against the backdrop of the narratives of biblical
characters like Joseph, Jacob and Leah, Gideon...the story shows
how the amazing favour of God intervenes at the nadir of one's
experiences with the promise of hope and restoration beyond one's
wildest dreams.

*Yvonne Pat Wright, lay preacher and author of **From Spice to
Eternity: Discovering the Main Ingredients to a Life of
Fulfillment and Purpose***
London, England

This book is practical and insightful to the cognitive approach
with biblical directives as to know how God will work in your favor.
It is reassuring and refreshing to know that God acts for you
when your enemies act against you ... One powerful principle that
we can glean from this book is "know who your enemy is so that
you know who God has defeated in your life."

Reverend Joseph Wilson
Senior Pastor McLeansville First Baptist Church
McLeansville, North Carolina

In this splendid inspirational piece Pastor Boulton uniquely
blends human experience and biblical record, and in both instances
allows us to see God's favor in our life. Boulton challenges us to
look past the "haters" of the world to the "hedge" of God around
us.

Elder Maynard G. Yates
Senior Pastor Mt Lebanon Primitive Baptist Church
Waxahachie, Texas

Someone once said that great things come in small packages. In
this small package Pastor Bernard Boulton uses the pain and
difficulties of his own life and extrapolates examples from scrip-
ture to teach profound truths about the favor of God. This book is
a must have for your personal library.

Elder Joseph Mosley
Senior Pastor Banks Creek Primitive Baptist Church
Portal, Georgia

Paralleling his life growing up in Hough Community in Cleveland, Ohio, with great characters in Israel, Pastor Boulton has written a book made for easy reading that presents personal challenges for the reader. The path to God's favor sometimes seems unfair but walking in God's will is the divine equalizer. This book vividly shows us how God's favor is with us when we seem unfavorable.

Harold E. Batts
Director of Development and Institutional Research
J.F. Drake State Technical College
Huntsville, Alabama

The vision outlined in this book can revolutionize and empower the church all over the world to take cities and nations for God and help them understand how the favor of God can operate in the lives of believers.

Reverend Dr. Rufus Fuller III
East New Hope Missionary Baptist Church
Danville, Virginia

Pastor Boulton has discovered a method of presenting the Gospel that is both enjoyable and edifying. **Divine Favor** is a tool for personal devotion as well as corporate Bible Study. It is replete with relevant insights for every reader.

Pastor Rodney Petty Sr.
Senior Pastor Life Church
Mesquite, Texas

Transformative, transparent, inspiring and informative are just a few words that articulate the dynamics of this treasure. In this book Bernard Boulton uses biblical motifs and interprets them based on his own personal and ministerial experiences. From the ancient biblical narratives that are loved and cherished by many, Boulton shows us how pain pushes us to our purpose and produces prosperity. This book will encourage, enlighten, and equip you as you journey through the author's journeys and gain insight.

Elder Jacques Moody, M. Div.
Senior Pastor, New Bethel Progressive Primitive Baptist Church
Ridgeway, Virginia

Divine Favor by Pastor Bernard Boulton is an eye-opener to the often difficult to understand dynamics of human conflicts and relationship. His transparent approach and thorough biblical examples help the reader gain insight into important practical applications of the divine favor of God. This book gave me hope to view relationships and circumstances through a different lens that in the end God intends for His favor to be manifested in our lives.

Scott Shafer, author of **What Every Dream Means**
San Diego, California

Divine Favor juxtaposes between the lives of biblical characters and Pastor Boulton's life. This story will definitely encourage many. It is well written and well thought out. My favorite chapter was the story of Leah.

Amos Johnson Jr. PhD
The Christian Entrepreneur Show
Atlanta, Georgia

The transparency of your journey in ministry is so refreshing that I have encouraged the young ministers that come through my Discipleship/Mentoring Ministry to read your story, especially those who have pastoral callings.

Your story tracks God's Divine Favor at every turn in your journey, even though it might have required looking back to discern it. Maybe others will be enlightened enough to discern the favor of God on their journey through your sharing.

Thank you, Scribe of God!

Prophetess Marion Clark Ingram / Founder-Director
Kingdom Institute
Memphis, Tennessee

Author: **Without Apology: On Call For God**
His Daughters Do Prophesy

DIVINE FAVOR

God Acts For You When Your Enemies Act Against You

Bernard Boulton

Riverlife Publishing Company

Divine Favor
God Acts for You When Your Enemies Act Against You

Copyright 2009 by Riverlife Publishing Company
P.O. Box 941, Danville, Va 24543

www.bernardboulton.com
www.facebook.com/pabernardboulton

Cover image: Emlyn Addison, www.ixwa.com
Source: Morguefile.com

Portrait Image: True Image Photography
Daniel Lovelace
4181 Rockford School Road
Gretna Va 24557

434-441-6878

ISBN 978-0-9859283-0-8

All rights reserved. No part of this book may be reproduced in any form or by any means without written consent of the Publisher. Published and printed in the United States of America.

A publication of Riverlife Publishing Company

"EVERYTHING WILL LIVE WHEREVER THE RIVER GOES."
Ezekiel 47:9 NKJV

Extracts from the Authorized Version of the Bible (The King James Bible), the rights in which are vested in the Crown, are reproduced by permission of he Crown's Patentee, Cambridge University Press.
Scriptures taken from the New King James Version. Copyright 1982 by Thomas Nelson, Inc. Used by permission. All rights reserved.

Dedication

Many years ago the Holy Spirit gave me the revelation that birthed this book. As I began to write what the Holy Spirit taught me in His classroom, I struggled. I wrote the introduction and chapters but the story was not flowing as I knew it should. One day I was talking with a spiritual brother at church about the writing and he said very forcefully, "Put yourself in it!" That was a word straight from God. I was writing a story about Divine Favor but it wasn't my story. *That* was the story I was sent to write. The brother was Minister Ricardo Oliver, associate minister, New Sardis Primitive Baptist Church, Cleveland, Ohio. I dedicate this story in his memory because Ricardo pushed me to tell the story you hold in your hand today.

I also dedicate this book to my wife Vantoria. When I thought I had completed writing the book, she said 'no, I had not.' Again the Holy Spirit spoke to me and showed me I needed to include more of my life from my childhood and adulthood. At this point I was led to include in this story a very humiliating season I didn't want to share. But I submitted to the Holy Spirit, and to the strategic counsel of my wife, to complete this story.

I dedicate this book to these two persons who have blessed my life and counseled me in the development of this book, Minister Ricardo Oliver (b Feb 15, 1953, d January 7, 2008) and my queen for 21 years on July 13, 2012, Vantoria Boulton.

Foreward

If there is one thing the remnant of the Lord has need of on a consistent basis, it is encouragement. God-inspired encouragement gives life and offers fuel for the continuation of the journey. It blows into dry bones and clears away fallen trees, mudslides and rocks that block the road. It pours fresh, healing oil on open wounds and it sutures them. It renews our Joy in the Lord as we are strengthened in its presence.

Bernard Boulton's recent release, **Divine Favor: God Acts for You When Your Enemies Act Against You** offers that type of encouragement-especially for those who find themselves falsely accused or Christly-accused as Father has revealed to me; and fighting for their very lives in the midst of traps set by the enemy of our God.

Boulton begins **Divine Favor** by sharing a chapter from his life as a young pastor in which his intentions to help others are sabotaged by accusations and gossip causing him to be accused of being everything, as the old folks would say, except a man of God. The slanderous assaults came from the very leaders and congregation he pastored.

They impacted him so much that they left him broken, deeply wounded, hopeless and discouraged not only in his calling to shepherd, but in his views of himself as a man, and a person.

I was able to fully identify with Boulton's journey, as I am sure many of you who read this book will as well. As I read, Father began to uncover hidden unforgiveness in my own heart. In one case, I had to go back over five years and release some things that I didn't realize I was still holding. It was a hurt buried in me beyond measure, and I thought Holy Spirit had dug it up and demolished it. As Father's chosen reconcilers we must face this simple truth. The enemy of our souls will go to great lengths to sabotage our destiny in the Lord. One of the most effective strategies he implements is discouragement – the deliberate murder of one's spirit. He goes after the spiritual jugular – our very identity in Christ.

While Boulton tastefully shares snapshots of his healing journey, each developing chapter focuses on showing the reader that even in the most difficult of situations the Lord is consistently, steadily, and forcefully working on our behalf to "awaken us to DIVINE FAVOR."

There is an earnest cry of intercession behind every chapter and journaling exercise in this book that will challenge those reading (1) to see themselves as Father sees them; (2) to believe that the Lord will never abandon them even when man does; (3) to trust that all things work together for their good – regardless of what the natural realm may present.

Apostle Theresa Harvard Johnson,
Founder of Voices of Christ Literary Ministries
International, Author of The Scribal Anointing
Atlanta, Georgia

Table of Contents

Introduction

Psalm 23:5: "Thou preparest a table before me in the presence of mine enemies" (King James Version).

The member voiced his complaint to the deacon as the two men spoke on the telephone. "That pastor that we done brought to this church is up to no good. Somebody called me and told me that he's using the church van to carry women around. You deacons need to do something."

A group from the church, along with the pastor, was in another city attending a convention. The pastor was new to the church and lies started circulating about him soon after his arrival. None of the deacons were at the convention, so they investigated the accusation that the deacon received from the member via telephone. None of the other members attending the convention could corroborate the story, although a few had their own stories to tell.

"I don't know about him carrying women around," one of the members told a deacon, "but he was hanging around with Pastor Jones, and you know I heard that Jones is on drugs. Even though I haven't seen our pastor doing drugs, you know they say that birds of a feather flock together."

When the pastor returned home from the convention, the deacons asked him to meet with them to tell him what some of the members were saying about him. The chairman of the deacons wanted to tell the pastor who his accusers were, but the pastor discouraged him from doing so.

The pastor left the meeting shaking his head, confused about what he was going through. He had only been at the church for three months and he was already embroiled in tensions he had only rarely experienced in his last pastorate.

The lies poisoned the church's relationship with the new pastor and soon they were spreading throughout the community. Other pastors started avoiding him. Fortunately he had made two friends in the city. In spite of what others were saying, those two remained his friends. The pressure from broken relationships and unresolved issues in the church took its toll on the pastor. Many Sundays during that year he would go to the church stressed and anxious, but when he ministered, God always gave him peace and the ability to show love to his enemies. God showed him favor by blessing his finances and he prospered more than he had ever prospered in his life. God favored him by anointing him to preach with power and to teach with clarity, and the church grew even in that toxic atmosphere. During that time, God released favor on him and his family. God prepared a table before him in the presence of his enemies. Finally, he left the church and the city where he and his family had moved a year before. He left severely wounded and disillusioned with the church.

After he left that church, he experienced favor in unlikely places. In the season of his wilderness, God continued to show him favor. He faced a lot of setbacks, and the life he lived was a hard one, but he lived it under the favor of God. And in that season of favor he learned new revelations about God that formed him into a different person. He learned that when his enemies attacked him, they were setting him up to experience the favor of God.

This is my story. I am that pastor I just told you about. I know I'm not alone in what I faced. Many of you reading these words have your own story to tell.

Your situation may be similar to mine.

He Went Through to Come Through

One evening I was at home watching *Praise the Lord* telecast on TBN. One of the guests was Bishop Hezekiah Walker. Bishop Walker was sharing about attacks that were leveled at him and lies that were spread about him. The Bishop talked about how painful it was when people believed lies told about him and even added their own lies. I could relate with his pain because I, too, had been there. Maybe not at the same level, but still I had walked through that valley. In that season, God showed Bishop Walker favor. Bishop Walker even sang a song on his CD *Souled Out*, titled "God Favored Me." This song is a testimony of Bishop Walker's experience. Let these words speak to your spirit as they speak to mine every time I hear them.

"I know you favored me because my enemies did try, but couldn't triumph over me...They whispered, conspired, they told their lies. God favors me."

And God favors you as He favored me and as He favored Bishop Hezekiah Walker. Bishop Walker went through to come through. After the season is over, God will bring you into a wealthy place (Psalm 66:12, KJV).

We've Got Company

Long before I went through my seasons of hurt and pain, and many years before Bishop Hezekiah Walker was the target of lies and attacks, there was one who went through a season of hate. His name was David. The king whom David loved and served wanted to murder him. Without provocation David's king became David's enemy. In that dark time in David's life, he received a revelation and an experience he shared with

14

us in Psalm 23:5: "Thou preparest a table before me in the presence of mine enemies" (KJV). David experienced favor from God. He called favor a table. See the picture in your mind. David is surrounded by his enemies. They want his life, but God made a table for David. The table is a place of protection. It is a place of provision. It is a place of peace. At the table, God protected David from King Saul. Many times, Saul and his armies of thousands got so close to David that they would have seized him and killed him had it not been for the protection of God. When God releases favor on you, His favor will protect you and you will have a Psalm 91 experience:

"I will say of the Lord, He is my refuge and my fortress; My God, in Him I will trust. Surely He shall deliver me from the snare of the fowler and from the perilous pestilence" (New King James Version).

When God favors you, He will deliver you from the will of your enemies. He will give you a strategy that causes you to bypass your enemy's designs. He will open a door of deliverance for you to walk right through the enemy's territory. While your enemy is trying to destroy you, God will provide for you. He will give you everything you need to make it and overcome. While you are facing your enemy and warring against your enemy, God will give you peace. You will find yourself calm in what appears to be your end.

Through many seasons in my life and ministry I have experienced this kind of favor. Through the spiritual impartation of the Holy Spirit, I have learned that favor is God reacting to me when man acts against me. I believe that this book, written from the premise of this revelation, is going to bless you tremendously. Through the trying of my faith, I have learned this timeless truth about the favor of God.

As you read these words, my prayer for you is this:

Holy Spirit, let these words breathe life into the persons who read them. May these words edify their spirit and release them to experience Your favor. Amen.

Chapter One

Favor When No One Loves You

Genesis 29–30

Leah was the oldest daughter of Laban. She loved
her father but she wasn't sure her father loved her.
Leah grew up in a culture where being a daughter
wasn't an advantage. Daughters were despised and
viewed as worthless. Socially they were held in the
same class as household servants. In Leah's world,
it was very rare for a daughter to be approved by her
father unless he could marry her off and receive a siz-
able dowry, or what was called a bride's price.

Leah was the eldest of two daughters; she had a
younger sister named Rachel. Rachel was a very beautiful woman and everyone assumed that Rachel would
marry a great and wealthy man. But no one had those
thoughts about Leah. Leah was looked upon with
pity—as the daughter with no future.

Imagine Leah living in your community, or Leah
being a member of your family. What would you say
about Leah? Would you make remarks like these?

"Poor Leah, she's probably never going to be married. Her daddy will have to take care of her until she dies."

"Leah sure is ugly. Who in their right mind would want to be with her?"

How do you think Leah would feel if she heard people talking about her in that manner? Can you identify with Leah? Have you ever been devalued and written off because of your physical appearance? Do you have low self-esteem because of what you have heard others say about you?

Growing Up with a Leah Complex

I was born in 1967 in Cleveland, Ohio. I was raised in a community called Hough. It was named after the first couple that settled there in 1799. Their names were Oliver and Eliza Hough. Hough became famous throughout the United States in July 1966, when the owner of a bar refused to serve a black woman. A crowd of protesters gathered outside the bar, and when the police showed up, a physical conflict ensued. Five days later, when the riots were over, four African Americans had been killed and 30 people had been injured. Two hundred and seventy-five arrests had been made and 240 fires had destroyed large sections of this already declining community.

The riots created an environment of despair and disillusionment for the residents who were left. It was in this community where I first came to know about life. Unfortunately, the environment of my surroundings influenced me. For most of my childhood, the community in which I lived shaped my worldview. Statistics suggested because I was born poor and black to a single mother, I would be a risk to the society at large. I would be a liability, possibly ending up in jail or dead before my 21st birthday. I had doubts in my soul that I would ever amount to anything. I had beliefs that had been planted in my mind that I would always be poor, always struggling, and always on the bottom trying to fight whatever it was holding me down. I was defeated, mentally, before I ever had to fight my first battle.

The environment of my community was the first enemy in my life. It was a community of broken down houses and trash-littered lots. It was a community of women raising their children without the benefit of a man's presence and support.

My environment, my community, produced low self-esteem in me. Like Leah, I thought very little of myself.

But even here, God showed me favor by giving me the ability to dream and a love of reading. Reading became my table in the presence of a community that was my enemy. As I matured, reading increased my intelligence, which eventually replaced my low self-esteem.

In part because of my own experience, the life of Leah came alive for me. This is how I view her story.

Leah and Jacob

One day Leah saw a stranger walking through the gate of their village. His name was Jacob. He was the son of Rebekah, Laban's sister, and Leah's aunt. Rebekah left home a long time ago to marry Isaac, a very wealthy distant relative. Jacob was the progeny of Rebekah and Isaac's union. As he strolled through the village, the tall handsome stranger turned the heads of many women in the village, including Leah. He strolled through the village as if he were a prince. Jacob created an impression in Leah's eyes. She could tell from the moment that she laid eyes on him that he was unlike any of the men in her village, including her father or any of her brothers. Leah fell in love with Jacob at first sight. Unfortunately for Leah, Jacob fell in love too, but not with her. Instead, Jacob fell head over heels in love with Leah's sister, Rachel.

Jacob went to Laban and asked for his daughter's hand in marriage. Laban agreed to give Rachel to Jacob if he worked seven years for the privilege to have her as his wife. Jacob agreed. For seven years Leah loved and watched this unusually handsome and quiet man from a distance. She longed to be the object of his affections. Leah watched with envy as Jacob courted Rachel. She saw the love in Jacob's eyes as he spent quiet moments with Rachel by the village well. Leah could hear his gentle voice as he declared his undying love for Rachel and spoke the vision of their future life together. Leah yearned to experience that kind of love with this man. She wanted Jacob in her life. She wanted Jacob to share his love and his hope with her, not with her sister.

When the seven years were complete, the village prepared for a wedding. Jacob and Rachel would be joined together. Or so everyone thought, including Leah.

The morning of the wedding feast Laban called Leah to his tent. Leah walked through the open tent flap and bowed before her father, showing her honor to him. Then she rose keeping her eyes cast downward. It was disrespectful for a woman to look directly at a man. Laban sat in the center of the tent surrounded by his sons.

"Leah I want you to marry Jacob," Laban said.

Leah was astonished. She kept quiet as Laban continued speaking.

"Tonight you will be given to Jacob as his wife, not your sister Rachel. You will be covered in a heavy marriage shroud. After the blessings have been given over you two, you will go into the marriage tent and wait for Jacob, your husband. Be sure that you don't speak to him at all so he will not discover you are not Rachel. By the time he realizes who you are, the marriage will be consummated."

Leah was astonished at her Father's words. She was dizzy with fear and excitement. How could she be a party to her father's deception? How could she perpetrate this wrong on Jacob? She doubted his plan could succeed. The more she thought about it, the more she became afraid of what Jacob would do to her when he discovered he had been deceived and cheated from marrying his true love. She didn't believe for a moment Jacob would be fooled. Leah knew he would know she wasn't Rachel. But no matter how she wanted to say no, she could not. She had to obey her father even if she believed Jacob was too cunning to fall for the trap being set for him.

That evening after the ceremony was over and the wedding feast was going on outside, Leah sat in the dark tent waiting for Jacob to appear. Her nerves were in a state of confusion and she was about to faint when Jacob finally entered the tent. She could tell that he was very drunk and not just from the wine. He was drunk with desire for the woman for whom he had waited the last seven years. Leah was mentally prepared to run when Jacob discovered who was waiting for him. She surmised that even though he was full of wine he would know the woman he held in his arms was not Rachel.

Jacob sat down next to Leah and took her in his arms. He removed the veil from her face and kissed her. To her joy he never found out who was with him on that night of marriage. She only felt slightly guilty as he whispered the name of Rachel in her ear.

Leah's joy turned to grief in the morning when Jacob awakened from his drunken stupor and discovered who he had been with the night before.

Jacob recoiled as he shouted, "Leah what are you doing here? Where is my Rachel?"

Leah bowed her head, saying nothing.

"What are you doing here, Leah?" He screamed at her as he ran around the tent frantically putting on his clothes.

After he dressed himself, he grabbed her and started shaking her. He was furious and Leah was sure he was going to kill her.

"Answer me!" He yelled shaking her with his strong hands.

Then Leah yelled out in fear, "You and I were married yesterday, not you and Rachel."

He threw her to the ground; she landed on the bed where they had consummated their marriage. Towering over her, Jacob raised his hand to strike her.

"You're lying," he yelled, the veins in his forehead bulging from his fury. "I was wed to Rachel yesterday!"

"No, my lord. You were wed to me yesterday."

He staggered backward. Turning away from Leah, he ran from the tent.

"Where is my wife? Where is Rachel?" Jacob yelled at Laban as he entered Laban's tent.

Laban spoke quietly to his enraged nephew. Laban's sons, who surrounded their father, all stood and looked menacingly at Jacob. They were ready to protect their father if they needed to. "You married Leah yesterday, not Rachel. It is not the custom in our country for the younger to marry before the eldest."

"I know nothing about your custom," Jacob yelled as he shook his finger at his uncle. "I worked seven years for Rachel to be my wife. You cheated me!"

Laban nodded his head at Jacob and invited him to

sit down. Jacob refused his offer and continued standing. "You can still have Rachel. Just stay with Leah for the week of marriage and I will give you Rachel."

"What's the catch Laban? I see it in your eyes," Jacob replied.

Smiling, Laban said, "Agree to work for me another seven years and Rachel is yours."

Jacob bowed his head. He knew that Laban had him right where he wanted him. Jacob loved Rachel and wanted her desperately. Defeated, Jacob said yes to Laban's request.

The week of marriage was a nightmare for Leah. Jacob despised her and his hostile attitude broke her heart.

Eight days after she and Jacob were married, Leah watched her husband marry her sister. The love and affection she wanted for herself from Jacob was gladly given to Rachel.

When Jacob visited Leah, he never showed her any love or affection. He never spoke warm words to her. He never held her in his arms. He never told her he loved her.

Leah's Favor from God

Leah wanted Jacob's love but she was about to encounter love from an unknown person, Jacob's God. She didn't know this God who saw her in her pain and rejection. God saw that Jacob didn't love Leah. God saw Leah used and despised by her husband, and God did something for her. God gave Leah favor. The God, who revealed Himself to Jacob's grandfather Abraham, came into her life to do more than she ever expected or wanted from her Jacob.

What did God do for Leah? He opened her womb. He chose her to bring into the world the first-born son of a new generation of Abraham's descendants.

Leah, the unloved wife, experienced the favor of God. God came into her life and blessed her beyond her wildest expectations. God treated her differently than Jacob treated her. At this stage in her marriage, Jacob was Leah's enemy and God was her defender.

You may be able to relate to Leah. Is it possible that you have been used and devalued by someone you love? You may be in a relationship where you are hated and despised, scorned, and ridiculed. If you are, start praising God for you are a prime candidate for God's favor. If He hasn't already, God is going to do something spectacular in your life because of how others have treated you. The people who have caused you pain have set you up for the favor of God. Praise God right now for His favor that is getting ready to do something in your life! There are doors God is about to open for you because of how you've been treated! Hallelujah!

Leah's life is a testimony to every person who has been unloved. God favored you or is about to favor you because there's a Jacob in your life who won't love you. Be encouraged by this truth: God will love you when Jacob won't!

One day Leah discovered she was pregnant. Months later she gave birth to a son. When her first son was born, Leah said, "The Lord has looked on my affliction. Now my husband will love me." She named her son Reuben, meaning, See a Son. Leah believed the birth of their first son would change Jacob's vision toward her, but it didn't.

When her second son was born, she named him Simeon. "Because the Lord has heard that I am unloved, He has given me this son."

Then Leah gave birth to a third son. "Now this time

my husband will come to me, because I have borne him three sons." She named him Levi.

The fourth son she named Judah as she declared, "Now I will praise the Lord."

At the birth of Judah, after years of bearing sons and trying to win the love of Jacob, Leah saw for the first time in her life the One who had always loved her; the One who was the source of her favor. When she recognized God's favor in her life, she praised God through the naming of her fourth son.

Favor is God saying, "I love you no matter how others may treat you." Favor is God treating you right when the people you love treat you wrong.

Leah received a revelation of God when she gave birth to Judah. Judah, her fourth son, was born from her body. But praise, the meaning of her son's name, was conceived in her spirit and she birthed that praise out of her mouth. Even as she went through natural labor to bring her fourth son into the earth, I believe Leah went through a spiritual labor to bring forth praise. Judah was a gift to Jacob, but her praise was a gift to God. The God she had discovered was the cause of favor in her life. She held Judah in her arms but she held praise in her heart. She responded to the God who had years earlier responded to her.

Every time Leah said Judah's name, she was also speaking the favor she recognized. God's love set Leah free from her history and from her loveless marriage.

If you are unloved, see God's favor in your life and get a praise in your mouth.

"I will praise the Lord even if my husband doesn't love me."

"I will praise the Lord even if my wife doesn't love me."

"I will praise the Lord in the presence of my enemies."

When you set your will to praise the Lord because you recognize His favor in your life, you are declaring His love is greater than anyone's hate.

Leah was free to believe she didn't have to win Jacob because God had won her with His favor. Leah saw God in the four sons that she had given birth to. In the midst of your circumstances, there is something God wants to birth in you. That's why He has given you favor, even if you haven't recognized it. God wants you to see Him, not the one who is hurting you or rejecting you.

When Leah opened her mouth and said, "Now I will praise the Lord," she became a worshipper of God: the God of Abraham, Isaac, and Jacob. She left the gods of her father. She left the mistreatment of her husband. She found God in His favor toward her and she became a worshipper of the one, true, living God.

When God shows you favor it is because He wants you to respond to Him the only way you can, by worshipping Him. Leah's praise was an acknowledgement of God in her life. She finally recognized the source of her blessings and the one who loved her unconditionally.

Leah looked at her sons and heard God say, "I love you."

No matter what you face in your relationships, God wants you to see Him, and know He loves you. God will give you Judah when Jacob won't love you.

Questions for Discussion

1. Have you ever been in a relationship and you knew the other person didn't love you?

2. Have you ever deceived someone whom you loved?

3. Would you have agreed to Laban's terms if you were Jacob?

4. Have you ever seen God's favor while you were in a loveless relationship?

5. Have you ever stayed in a relationship hoping the person whom you loved would change their feelings toward you?

Chapter Two

Favor Is More Than a Coat

Genesis 37–50

Joseph was the eleventh son in a family of twelve boys. His father Jacob loved him more than he loved his other children. In a demonstration of his love, Jacob had a coat of many colors made for Joseph. The coat was a statement to everyone in the family that Joseph was the beloved son and the heir to Jacob's vast estate.

Joseph's Brothers

Unfortunately for Joseph, the coat made him a target of his brothers' hatred. They hated him so much it influenced their conversation with him. Genesis 37:4 says, "They could not speak peaceably to him" (NKJV). A person's words to you will always reveal a person's heart toward you. Your enemy will expose himself by what he says to you and about you.

The tension in the family escalated when Joseph

told his family about his two dreams.

"Please hear this dream which I have dreamed; There we were, binding sheaves in the field. Then behold, my sheaf arose and also stood upright; and indeed your sheaves stood all around and bowed down to my sheaf" (Genesis 37:6–7, NKJV).

Joseph's brothers were furious and said, "Shall you indeed reign over us? Or shall you have indeed dominion over us?" (Genesis 37:8, NKJV). Joseph's brothers hated him because of his dreams. What is astonishing is that Joseph dreamed the dreams, but his brothers interpreted the dreams. Although Joseph was gifted in having dreams, his brothers were equally gifted in interpreting dreams. They hated Joseph because of his dream and they couldn't celebrate their ability to know what the dream meant. Their gift of interpretation was just as important as Joseph's revelation. It was Joseph's brothers who revealed his destiny, the destiny Joseph may not have known at that time. Many times the people who hate you already know what God has ordained for you. They hate you because they know what God is showing you. Not only have you seen your dreams, but also your haters have seen your dreams. They know what the dreams mean, and what you dreamed caused them to hate you.

Joseph had a second dream, which he told to his father and brothers. "Look I have dreamed another dream. And this time, the sun, the moon, and the eleven stars bowed down to me" (Genesis 37:9, NKJV).

Joseph's brothers envied him as well as hated him. Hate and envy is a dangerous combination. Because the brothers hated Joseph, it affected their feelings toward him. Envy caused them to desire what Joseph had.

Hate disconnected the brothers from Joseph. It put them on opposite sides. Hate infected their conversation. It caused them to be blind to the fact that they, too, had a covenant with God, like their great-grandfather Abraham. They couldn't appreciate who they were because they wanted to be who Joseph was.

Don't be like Joseph's brothers. Celebrate who you are in Christ. Don't be envious of others who may appear to have more than you. Thank God for what you have and for who you are. You have a destiny. You have a future. God has plans for you. Don't envy the Josephs in your life. Celebrate the Josephs in your life. Be the Joseph in your life. If you can't be the dreamer, then be the interpreter of the dreams.

One day Jacob sent Joseph to Dothan to find out how his brothers were doing. As Joseph approached the camp where they were, his brothers conspired to kill him. "Look the dreamer is coming! Come therefore, let us now kill him and cast him into some pit; and we shall say, 'Some wild beast has devoured him.' We shall see what will become of his dreams!" (Genesis 37:19–20, NKJV).

When Joseph arrived in the camp, his brothers grabbed him, stripped the coat off of him, and threw him into a pit. When they stripped the coat off of Joseph, they were taking the symbol of their father's favor from Joseph. Initially they wanted to kill Joseph, but after listening to Reuben, the eldest brother, they decided to sell him to a band of traders. When they returned home, they told their father Joseph was dead.

Joseph Finds Favor in an Unlikely Place

The brothers of Joseph acted against him, and their actions caused God to act with favor toward Joseph. Through his brothers' hate, God moved Joseph to the place that positioned him in the kingdom of Egypt, where his dreams would one day manifest.

Joseph's experience may be your experience. You may have encountered hatred and betrayal by members in your own family. You may have experienced hatred and betrayal by members of the church where you belong. The hatred of others is often an opportunity for you to be positioned for God's favor to be manifested in your life. You ought to praise God for your Joseph experience!

Joseph's Brothers Live

In February 1984, I acknowledged God had called me into the ministry. The news spread throughout my community and my high school. And almost immediately I encountered my first Joseph brother. He and I were good friends. Several times a week we were together playing basketball at the outside basketball court of our high school, and we would meet at another playground to play basketball or just hang together, doing what teenage boys did. But our camaraderie ended when he heard I was going to start preaching. His attitude changed toward me and he started to taunt me daily in school when we had lunch together. He would assault me with words like these:

"You ain't no preacher. Who do you call yourself? I know you. God ain't call you to preach. I guess you gonna be one of them money hustling preachers."

Every day for weeks he would verbally attack me at school and on the basketball court. Of course, I understood the reason for his hostility toward me. My friend had a hostile demeanor toward religion and it didn't help that I didn't always represent Jesus like I should. Profanity and cursing were normal expressions of language where we played ball and where teens congregated, and I could curse with the best of them. So in my friend's eyes I was about to become a hypocrite.

Until I confessed that God had called me to preach, I was never one to aggressively witness to anyone I knew who might not have the same belief as I. I would tell people about the Lord only when the Lord came up in our conversation, which was very rare.

After about six weeks, I had had enough of him and I threw some food in his face. When he jumped out of his seat, I turned the table over on him. When he came at me brandishing his fist, I hit him and he fell to the floor. That was the week before I was to preach my initial sermon. I was suspended from school; it was my first suspension in eleven years of attending public schools. My friend was the first in a long line of Joseph brothers in my life.

A member of my family also expressed animosity. One day before I preached my first sermon, one of my cousins said to our grandmother, "Bernard ain't been called to preach. He's been in his room listenin' to those preacher records and now he thinks that he can preach like that man."

The man he was talking about was the late Reverend C. L. Franklin. Reverend Franklin was one of the most popular preachers in America. He had attained fame through the sales of his sermonic records. Even before I started preaching, I would listen to his sermons on the radio and I would eventually own dozens of his records.

One day my cousin said to me, "I was supposed to be the preacher in our family, not you."

Words like his, and taunts like the ones my friend so freely expressed, hurt me and angered me. But as I learned in ministry, attacks based on envy and jealousy were opportunities for God to show me favor as he showed Joseph.

No matter where Joseph was or what Joseph experienced, the word of God said, "The LORD was with

Joseph" (Genesis 39:2, NKJV). Favor comes from the presence of God. God's presence released favor in Joseph's life. The fruit of favor is prosperity and that's what Joseph experienced as a slave in Egypt. What an astonishing truth — Joseph became prosperous in slavery! Genesis 39:2 says Joseph was successful. Verse 3 says the Lord made all that Joseph did "to prosper."

Favor is God's presence coming into your situation to make something good happen for you. Joseph was familiar with favor because he was the favored son of his father, Jacob. But now in slavery, Joseph experienced favor greater than his father's favor! He experienced the favor of God! He was living in a strange land, but he had favor! God broke through Joseph's bondage and made things happen for him. Joseph was promoted while he was a slave in another man's house! Joseph was in bondage, but favor made Joseph free.

You may despise your life and your circumstances as you read these words. You may hate your current place, but hold on to this truth. God is with you. If you receive this truth in your heart and confess it out of your mouth, you will succeed where you are! Just confess right now out of your mouth, "Where I am right now God is with me!"

Favor will get you promoted – even when it seems impossible. Joseph the slave became Joseph the overseer of the house. Favor caused him to thrive in the worst situation of his life.

Because you are a child of God, you can overcome your worst situation by the favor of God. God will enable you to overcome your enemies and overcome your situations. That dead end job you believe is the end of the road can be overcome. Where there is a wall and it seems you can't get over it, by the favor of God you can leap over it!

That life of poverty and lack you are experiencing right now, can be overcome because God is with you!

I Found Favor!

In the summer of 2001, I resigned from the church where I was pastoring. Mentally, I was through with pastoral ministry. I packed up my family and I returned home to Ohio, eight years after we had left for me to pastor in West Virginia. I had been diagnosed as clinically depressed. I was taking medication every day. I had gone through a major spiritual storm that ruined my health and darkened my vision. I was not sure I would ever return to full-time ministry as a pastor. I came out of the storms alive, but wounded.

By the beginning of October, I had completed my last preaching assignment for the year. I needed to find work to continue providing for my family. I had been in full-time ministry since 1993. My résumé and job qualifications were primarily pastoral ministry and preaching. I went to a job placement center to get help in finding work.

The woman who managed the office said to me, "You'll never find a good job with this kind of work experience. Everybody's going to be worried that you are going to come in and try to preach to them. I suggest that you find yourself a church, Reverend."

I didn't care what she said, and I definitely wasn't interested in getting a church. So I kept on looking for employment and within the week I was hired with a security company. I lived in Northeast Ohio for six years and during that period I continued to preach and teach in churches throughout the Midwest. God showed me favor by giving me a position with a company and giving me opportunities to minister His word.

When you have been pushed into a situation,

believe God is going to release His favor in your life. You may have lost your lucrative position and where you are now is not where you saw yourself. You may have gone through a painful divorce that left you broken. God is going to favor you and you will succeed in the place where you land.

God's favor was not limited to Joseph, but flowed throughout Potiphar's house because Joseph lived there. The blessing of the Lord was on Potiphar's house and his field because of Joseph. When God favors you, He will also give favor to those who you work for or work with. Your presence in that workplace is bringing the presence of God there, which is releasing the favor of God in that place. I don't care if you work at a hamburger stand, God is with you in the hamburger stand, and favor is in that place because you are there. God will bless others because you are in their life. Because you are a member of that church, God's favor is there.

When Favor Ran Out Again

In the midst of favor Joseph faced another enemy. This time it was a woman—his master's wife.

"And it came to pass after these things that his master's wife cast longing eyes on Joseph, and she said 'lie with me' " (Genesis 39:7, NKJV).

God's favor will attract people to you who have the desire to cause you to compromise your values, causing you to lose God's favor in your life. When you are experiencing favor, you have to be cautious of the people who appear in that season. The enemy of your soul will move people to you who have a demonic assignment. That assignment is to cause you to step away from the manifest presence of God so you will lose the favor of God and everything you have gained from His favor.

It breaks my heart to think about the moral failure of people who were greatly favored by God, whom God had exalted and brought out of the world, and upon whom God bestowed His favor in their lives. They had overcome enemies and betrayals and attacks only to finally fall to the enemy's schemes of sexual indiscretions. And although it is true that God will not turn His back on you when you fall into sin, it is also true that sin stops the flow of God's favor in your life. The enemy hates favor and will do everything to stop it from flowing in your life.

Potiphar's wife tried to seduce Joseph, but he overcame sexual temptation.

"But he refused and said to his master's wife, 'Look my master does not know what is with me in his house, and he has committed all that he has to my hand. There is no one greater in this house than I, nor has he kept back anything from me but you, because you are his wife. How then I can I do this great wickedness, and sin against God?' " (Genesis 39:8–9, NKJV).

Joseph overcame the advances of Potiphar's wife, but he couldn't overcome her lies.

And so it was, when she saw that he had left his garment in her hand and fled outside, that she called to the men of her house and spoke to them, saying, "See, he has brought in to us a Hebrew to mock us. He came in to me to lie with me, and I cried out with a loud voice. And it happened, when he heard that I lifted my voice and cried out, that he left his garment with me, and fled and went outside." (Genesis 39:13–15, NKJV).

For the second time in his life, Joseph's coat is stripped off him. Joseph's season in Potiphar's house was over and he was forced to move to the next place— prison. Genesis 39:21–23 says, "But the LORD was with Joseph and showed him mercy, and He gave him favor in the sight of the keeper of the prison...and whatever he did, the LORD made it prosper" (NKJV). Joseph was in a different place, but again, because of the actions of his enemies against him, Joseph experienced the favor of God.

You Can Overcome Life; Don't Let Life Overcome You

Joseph was in prison but he didn't become bitter. Bitterness would have cut off the flow of favor operating in his life. Bitterness is destructive because it destroys the person and corrupts his heart, destroying his favor. Joseph knew that God was with him and this kept him going while he was in prison. He trusted the same God who had been with him since he was brought to Egypt in chains. God didn't disappoint him, but blessed him tremendously. He would not sin against his God by giving in to the sexual advances of his master's wife, and he would not allow his heart to become polluted with bitterness. Joseph went to prison because a woman lied about him, but in prison he found favor. It doesn't matter where you are when you have God's favor. You can have His favor in the worst places.

Let Favor – Not Your Circumstances – Define You

Favor will make you look different to people. Joseph did not look like a prisoner even though he was in prison! In the eyes of the jailer, Joseph looked different. No matter how you think you look, the favor of God will make you look different. The people whom God set in your path will not see you in confinement. They will see you in favor. Some of you don't look like the place where you are! People have been telling you that you don't belong where you are because they see you in a different light. That light is God's favor! God will cause people to see you differently so that they will acknowledge where God has already ordained you to be.

Joseph was given authority in the prison because there were two men coming to the prison, and one of those men would be the bridge to Joseph fulfilling his destiny. In prison, Joseph had room to operate because of favor. When you receive favor from God it doesn't matter where you are, God will give you room.

God Gave Me Room!

I was in a narrow place in my life and God gave me the word from Genesis 26:22 that there's room in Rehoboth. Isaac went through a series of battles and setbacks until he discovered a place called Rehoboth. God gave Isaac favor there. Prison became Rehoboth for Joseph; he had room to operate in his gifts. He had room to grow.

I've met believers who rejected what others saw in them because they couldn't see it in themselves. I've seen women who were beautiful women, but rejected compliments because they couldn't see what others saw. I've seen men who have greatness within them and they reject encouragement because they don't see in themselves what others saw in them. You need to find Rehoboth; you need room to see yourself!

When Joseph stood before Pharaoh in Genesis 42, he didn't stand as a slave and a prisoner. He stood before Pharaoh as a man with the favor of God. This favor caused Pharaoh to hear Joseph's words and his wisdom. It wasn't Joseph's intelligence, or his handsome features that caused Pharaoh to hear him; it was the favor of God on Joseph. Genesis 41:37 says, "So the advice was good in the eyes of Pharaoh..." (NKJV). Pharaoh saw something: he saw what the prison keeper saw; he saw what Potiphar saw; he even saw what Joseph's brothers saw and hated. Pharaoh saw favor and he responded to it by promoting Joseph and giving Joseph more than he ever had. The favor of God brought Joseph to his destiny—from his father's tent to Potiphar's house to prison to the throne of Egypt.

What God did for Joseph, He will do for you. Do not allow others to break the dreams God has placed in you. Every attack against you will release God's favor in your life and bring you to the place where God desires you to be.

Questions for Discussion

1. What is your opinion on parental favoritism?

2. Joseph's brothers envied him for his dreams. Have you ever envied a person?

3. How did favor manifest itself in Joseph's life while he lived with Potiphar?

4. What can stop favor from flowing in your life?

5. How did Joseph escape bitterness in prison? Have you ever been bitter?

Chapter Three

Favor In a Hiding Place

Judges 6–8

It was a terrible time for the people of Israel. Their enemies, the Midianites, were oppressing them terribly. Israel had become a nation of slaves under the harsh treatment of the Midianites. Throughout the country, people left their homes to live in caves, in a desperate attempt to find some relief from their enemies and protect their only resource, the harvest from their fields. Every year the Midianites descended on Israel and took their harvest—their only means of survival and the result of their hard work. Because of the Midianites' conquest, Israel was an extremely poor nation. Every spring Israel would sow their seeds in the hope that this year they would be able to keep their harvest, and at every harvest the Midianites would invade their villages and steal their harvest, leaving them destitute.

So it was equally true in the community of my childhood. By the time I was born and was growing up,

Hough was an impoverished community. But it wasn't always like that. At the turn of the twentieth century and during the historical period known as the "Roaring Twenties," Hough was a prosperous community. The Hough community was connected to Euclid Avenue, which was known as "Millionaire's Row." Some of the most elaborate houses and mansions were built on Euclid Avenue and in the Hough community. Names such as John D. Rockefeller, George Worthington, and Jephta Wade were among the wealthiest men in America who made Euclid Avenue their home. Because of the close proximity between Euclid and Hough, Hough became known as "Little Hollywood." It was a community of theatres and clubs. People from all over the city would go there for entertainment.

During the 1930s and 1940s, Hough became a community of middle class Europeans. In the 1950s, large numbers of blacks were moving in and whites were moving out. By 1960, 75 percent of Hough was African American. After the riots in 1966, the community that I knew was a community of poor living conditions and increasing joblessness. The policies of the welfare system drove many men from their homes, leaving women to raise the children.

The Hough of the 1970s, the Hough of my childhood, mirrored the conditions of Israel during the time of Judges. Poverty was persistent. Our community continued to deteriorate as crime increased. And there were very few people with hope in tomorrow. Most families were just struggling to survive and exist from day to day. As a young child, I watched my Mother struggle to provide for her children and take care of us. I never really knew the burden she was under until I was almost a grown man. Poverty was the Midianite in my young life—in my community. It was the pernicious enemy that kept rising against us, trying to defeat us and ultimately destroy us.

These words recorded in the sixth chapter of Judges describe the plight of Israel: "So Israel was greatly impoverished because of the Midianites, and the children of Israel cried out to the LORD" (Judges 6:6, NKJV). Israel knew why they were in the situation that they were in, and they knew how to get out. Judges 6:1 says, "Then the children of Israel did evil in the sight of the LORD. So the LORD delivered them into the hand of Midian..."

Whenever Israel turned away from God and did evil, God would turn them over to their enemies.

The Way Out

In spite of how you got to the place where you are right now, and in spite of what you're going through, you can call on the Lord right now and He will hear you. Sin may have brought you to where you are now and you may be suffering, but you can do what Israel did. If you call on the Lord now, if you cry out to God right now, He will give you favor. He will react to your situation and He will rise up against your enemies and give you favor.

God did it for me. I made it out of the environment of my childhood because as a little boy growing up at the Antioch Primitive Baptist Church, I learned how to cry out to God. I cried out to God to deliver me, to make my dreams come true, and He did it for me! I could have been like many of the young men with whom I grew up, went to school with, and even went to church with. I could have sought the answer to my first enemy, the environment that I grew up in, in the bottle like so many did. I could seek the answer by dropping out of school and waiting for a check and food stamps every month like so many did. I could have sought the answer by proving my manhood by getting several girls pregnant without having the maturity or economic stability to provide for them like so many did. But I sought another way.

I would go into my room and dream. I would dream about writing books and telling stories that would impact people. I would dream about traveling to places beyond my community and having different experiences. And then I would pray. I would ask God to make my dreams come true. God heard me and right now as I write these words, God is continuing to answer the prayers of that little boy from Hough.

But before you call on God to rescue you, there is a principle you need to receive from this biblical account. The principle is: Know who your enemy is so that you will know whom God has defeated in your life. In Judges 6:7 it says, "And it came to pass when the children of Israel cried out unto the LORD, because of the Midianites" (NKJV).

Do you know who your enemy is? Do you know the specific person or thing or situation oppressing you? Do you know who the agent of your trouble is? If you don't know, ask the Holy Spirit to reveal it to you so that when you cry out to God and He delivers you, you will know who or what He has delivered you from. Many times we seek deliverance and we don't know what we need to be delivered from. For some of you, the Midianite is a person that keeps you down because he or she speaks oppression to you. The Midianite may be a situation you refuse to leave, or even recognize for what it is. When you can name your enemy and ask God to deliver you, you are positioning yourself for the favor of God. And when He comes, He is going to free you from the Midianites and He's going to defeat your enemy at the same time.

During the time of Judges in Israel's history, God raised up a man named Gideon. Gideon could relate to what was happening in Israel, because it was happening to him. When God gave favor to Gideon, He also gave favor to Israel. When God favors you, He also gives favor to your community. Personal favor many times becomes corporate favor. Favor in your life becomes favor in your family. Favor in your family becomes favor in your community. When Gideon is introduced in Judges 6:11, he is hiding wheat in the winepress. Gideon was hiding his harvest from his enemies. The people of God were praying, and God's answer to their prayers was Gideon.

Favor began for Gideon as he heard the Word from God. The angel of the Lord said to Gideon in Judges 6:12, "The LORD is with you, you mighty man of valor!" (NKJV). The words of the angel of the Lord gave Gideon a new identity. In God's eyes, Gideon was a mighty man of valor. Before favor changes your circumstances, it first changes how you see yourself. The angel spoke personally to Gideon. It was a word that Gideon needed to hear to bring him into favor.

I Didn't See What God Says

As a child I had many complexes. Because of my dark complexion, other children in school and in the community often called me names. Those names formed my opinion of myself. As I grew, people would tell me how handsome or attractive I was. I wouldn't believe them because I believed what I was told as a child by other children. As a growing young man I dated several very attractive young women, but I never believed I was worthy of their company because I didn't believe I was their equal.

I never felt worthy of the gifts I received from my mother and grandmother. And later I had the same attitude concerning my fiancée and future mother-in-law who loved lavishing me with presents. I would try to dissuade them and they couldn't understand, because I couldn't explain to them I didn't feel worthy of their expressions of love toward me. I didn't believe I was worthy because I didn't believe what God said about me. I believed the names I was given by other children, but I couldn't believe what God said about me.

God said I was His child.

God said I was fearfully and wonderfully made.

God said I was the head and not the tail.

God said I was chosen, a royal priest, a member of a holy nation, special to Him.

Like Gideon I couldn't believe what God said about me.

Gideon could not see what God said about him because of what he saw happening to him and God's people. The angel told Gideon what God saw in him and who he would be. Gideon, however, could not see what the angel said to him because his vision was focused on his nation's present trouble and on its past and on his past. Gideon's reply to the angel's announcement to him was,

"O my lord, if the LORD is with us, why then has all this happened to us? And where are all His miracles which our fathers told us about...But now the LORD has forsaken us and delivered us into the hands of the Midianites." (Judges 6:13, NKJV).

In verse 12 the Lord appeared to Gideon and in verse 14 the Lord turned to him. First Gideon saw God and then God saw Gideon. And when God turned to Gideon, God said, "Go in this might of yours, and you shall save Israel from the hands of the Midianites" (Judges 6:14, NKJV).

When God turns to you, favor is manifested; it's

time to step out and be what God is calling you to be. When God turns to you, it's time to step into your purpose and do what God has ordained you to do.

It may be God's plan for you to rescue your family, or your community, from the oppression it is experiencing right now. By following His Word you are taking the first step in overcoming the oppressive identity you have believed and received in your spirit. Gideon had to be delivered from his own thinking before he could act on the word spoken to him.

God saw him as a mighty man of valor. God told him to go and save his people, but Gideon had issues that may have caused him to miss God's favor. Gideon had low self-esteem. "O my Lord, how can I save Israel? Indeed my clan is the weakest in Manasseh, and I am the least in my Father's house" (Judges 6:15, NKJV). Gideon had a poor vision of himself and his family. Gideon was a victim of the "Who Me?" syndrome.

Who, me, Lord?
You don't mean me, Lord, do you?
I'm not qualified to do that Lord.
Surely you can get someone else Lord.

An Enemy Called Lack

Most of my life I have known poverty. Sometimes it was the result of poor and unwise decisions. Other times, it was because of circumstances I could not control. But I never lacked as I did the year I was pastoring and on welfare.

Vantoria and I had quit our jobs and packed up to move to our first pastorate, believing this was the will of God. The small congregation of forty was excited to have us, and we were excited at the potential of the work there. Adding to my excitement was the rapid growth I had witnessed at the church where I was a member. New Sardis Primitive Baptist Church had increased by ninety members that year, and the men's class I was teaching had doubled from ten to twenty men. Vantoria and I were on fire for God, and God was blessing the church as it grew from forty members to sixty members. I had a group going with me to visit community members, new people were coming to the church, and old members were returning. For six months, everything was going well. Then it happened. Members became delinquent in their giving and the church soon was without money and unable to pay its bills – or me.

I started looking for a job, but there were no jobs for me. As the bills started to pile up and disconnection notices started to come in, one of the trustees came to me and said, "Pastor if you can't find a job, then you need to go and sign up for welfare."

I was astonished and stared at him, not believing what I had just heard him say.

"I'll never go on welfare. God's gonna take care of me and my family. We came here because He sent us here, and He will provide."

I was bothered by the suggestion, but what really troubled me was I was already contemplating welfare. The rent would soon be due and my savings account was empty.

I stayed up many nights before I made that journey to the welfare office, talking to God about my past and my history, about my childhood. I felt like I had been set up for a knock out. Had God brought me here to humiliate me? To put me in a position that would take me back to the place I had left so long ago? Was this a punishment for pride? I couldn't believe God would call me to a church 200 miles away from home and family, and then place me in such dire circumstances. I felt hurt and betrayed; all those years of serving, waiting, and preparing until God gave me a flock to shepherd and lead. Vantoria and I had stepped out on faith and *this* was our reward.

With no other avenues to explore, I walked with my head down to the welfare office to apply for assistance.

The worker who facilitated the process said, upon discovering I was a pastor in a local church, "Humph. Your church is supposed to take care of you Reverend."

I replied sarcastically, "Who's your Pastor?"

When she replied, I asked, "Are ya'll taking care of him? Is he a full-time pastor or does he have to work to take care of his family?"

Sheepishly she replied, "No, we don't do what we should for our pastor either."

I had some more choice words for her—words that shouldn't come from the mouth of a Man of God, so I contained them.

We were on welfare for six months until we left that community to come to the church where I am today. I didn't see it of course, but the enemy was against me. And God was for me, still showing favor to the pastor on welfare.

The angel of the Lord greeted Gideon and commissioned him to deliver the people from their enemy. And even though Gideon said, "Who, me?" God sent him and God used him. No matter how you see yourself, or believe you have nothing to offer God, God will give you favor to overcome what you believe about yourself.

God showed favor to His people through Gideon, and Gideon defeated the enemy. Israel enjoyed peace for forty years.

Questions for Discussion

1. Have you ever experienced poverty in your life? What did poverty look like?

2. Israel knew the cause of their poverty; do you know the cause of your poverty?

3. What was your way out of poverty?

4. Who does the Midianite represent in your life?

5. Do you believe what God says about you? List five things that God has said about you from His Word.

Chapter Four

Pushed Into Favor

1 Samuel 1

In the tribe of Ephraim in northern Israel, there lived a man named Elkanah and his two wives, Hannah and Peninnah. Peninnah had children and Hannah did not.

This family unit was in discord. They were divided. There was one man and two women, trying to live in the bounds of matrimony. There was trauma and drama in this house. There were two women loving and sharing one man. One wife had an edge over the other wife. Hannah had Elkanah's heart, but Peninnah had his children and she didn't fail to remind Hannah of this fact repeatedly.

These two women were enemies living together. Peninnah was the wife with the vindictive and malicious tongue. Hannah was the wife with the broken heart. Unknown to Hannah was the fact that God had not given her a level playing field. We read these words about Hannah in I Samuel 1:5, "the LORD had closed her womb" (NKJV). And in I Samuel 1:6, "And her adversary also provoked her sore, for to make her fret, because the LORD had shut up her womb" (KJV). Not only was Peninnah against Hannah, it seemed as if the Lord Himself was against her too. By closing Hannah's womb, God had given ammunition to Hannah's enemy to harass her.

I love this story because it reveals God will sometimes orchestrate your circumstances to get you to the point where He will release favor on you. What I'm saying is sometimes the person who is attacking you has been given the means to attack you so that God can favor you. That's awesome! That's God! He gives the ammunition to your enemy to attack you so He can turn around and bless you. Can you explain that? I can't, but I know that's how God operated in Hannah's life.

God puts the nails in the hands of your enemies to nail you to a cross and then watches them write your obituary. On your tombstone they write that you are finished. Then God will release His favor on you by calling you out of the grave they put you in, and show your enemy you were dead but now you are alive! When your Peninnah thought you were dead and buried, you came walking out of the grave a witness that God's favor brought you out!

You may now be asking why God doesn't just give me favor without my enemy harassing me. The harassment is an opportunity for you to grow so that when you receive favor, you will be mature enough to receive what God has for you. Opposition is like the penetrating heat of sun rays that beat down on the seed, calling it out of the ground so that it will grow for harvest. God's ways are not our ways, His thoughts are not our thoughts, but His favor is incredible!

Elkanah and his wives went to Shiloh every year to

worship. And even during this time, Peninnah would provoke Hannah.

Imagine this scene with me. Imagine Hannah and Peninnah together in church. Praise and worship is electrifying. Hannah is getting her praise on and Peninnah whispers in her ear, "Why are you praising Him like that? You're not going to ever have any babies with your barren self."

Can you hear Peninnah speaking loudly to Hannah as they go forward to give their tithes and offerings?

"What are you doing here? You keep on giving to God thinking that He's going to give you a baby. You can't buy God. What are you here in the temple for? Giving gifts to God with your barren self. You are a disgrace to our husband Elkanah—he may love you more but I got his babies."

It is one thing to be attacked, but to be attacked while you are worshipping God and giving Him the gifts due Him is harsh. There are times when your enemy will attack you while you are in the presence of God, worshipping Him.

The Pain of Waiting

I knew when I started preaching at the age of seventeen that God would one day place me to be a shepherd over His flock. I did what was necessary to prepare for that day. I was faithful as an associate minister to my spiritual Father. I followed every assignment He gave me and I had never accepted an invitation without His permission. The years passed and eventually I left the church where I grew up and joined the New Sardis Primitive Baptist Church. It was a hard adjustment having been in one church all of my life and then leaving to become a part of another church. But I held on to the conviction that I would one day become a pastor, a spiritual shepherd to the people of God. Then I started watching other ministers my age get pastoral assignments, when I didn't. After a while I started doubting what I believed I heard from God. The enemy would whisper in my ear that I would never pastor. I considered leaving my denomination to go to a denomination with more churches, increasing my chances for receiving a pastoral call. But God spoke to me through my second spiritual father, Elder Jimmie Warren, and I stayed. It wasn't easy to hold on to a promise that seemed unlikely to come to pass.

One of the pastors in my denomination told me my problem was I wasn't courting any churches. He said I had to treat a church like a woman and pursue her. I couldn't accept his line of thinking, so I waited. Every so often I heard my enemy repeat that it would never happen. Then, after nine years of waiting and preparing, God opened a door for me in Beckley, West Virginia. Like Hannah, I had to wait. It seemed like a long wait, but God used the devil's harassment and his intentional campaign to plant doubt in my mind to grow me so I was ready to receive what He had for me.

No matter how your enemy provokes you and speaks to you, don't stop going to Shiloh! Don't stop worshipping God.

One day Hannah went to the house of the Lord provoked and crying and upset and distraught. She couldn't eat but she kept going. And that's what you've got to do; no matter what you face and what you go through, you keep on going to His house to honor and praise Him.

Hannah kept going but she was affected by the war with her rival. She was affected by her life. The Bible says that one day she went to the tabernacle and she was "...in bitterness of soul" (I Samuel, 6:10, KJV). The continual harassment, the put downs, the verbal assaults, and the barrenness had formed bitterness in her soul. The significance of the change in her soul is punctuated by the meaning of her name. Hannah means grace. Once upon a time in her life, she lived her name. She walked in her destiny as a woman of grace. But now there's a change in Hannah, life had changed her and made her bitter.

Hannah, meaning grace, is now Hannah the bitter woman.

Hannah, who once spoke with grace on her lips, became a woman with anger dripping from her lips.

Hannah, who once celebrated others blessings, is now resentful of every woman in her life who has what she wants.

She goes to the temple with a new name, Hostile Hannah.

She stood in the presence of God with bitterness in her soul and released tears of anguish from her eyes. She went to prayer meeting not feeling like it, but she wouldn't be directed by her feelings. In spite of what was going on in her, she believed God would meet her at Shiloh.

The provocation of her enemy drove her to prayer meeting. But this time, this certain time was different because she did something different. She prayed and she made a vow, which was different. She asked God for a male child; she vowed to give the child to God, and God responded to Hannah's vow. God had closed her womb but He had a son for her. And her son was unlike any son born in his generation. God took her through all that drama to bring her to a point where she was moved to pray and make a vow. The vow Hannah made was a promise to give her son to the Lord. Hannah reached beyond herself and reached out to God, bringing Him into her situation and declaring by faith her intention to bless Him if He blessed her.

Hannah's Breakthrough

Something happened to Hannah when she prayed and made her vow to God. The bitterness fell off her soul like scales. She had regained her destiny as Grace.

Hannah had a breakthrough in her soul. What she felt when she entered the house of her God was no longer there. The first sign of God's favor to Hannah was the change inside of her. Before God gives you favor in your circumstances, He first shows you favor by changing what's going on inside of you.

A change in Hannah's soul caused a change in her behavior. A change in Hannah's behavior changed her marriage, and the next time she and her husband came together in intimacy, the Lord remembered her.

You may be facing great persecution and there may be a rival in your life who is frustrating you and giving you all kinds of grief. You may be bitter in your soul about your life and your marriage and your situation. I want to minister to you today and tell you to make yourself like Hannah. It may have been a long time since you have felt the presence of God in your soul. I'm calling you to make Hannah's story your story. It doesn't matter if you are a man or a woman, put yourself in her shoes and follow her example. Go before the Lord in prayer and make a vow. Make a promise to God. Declare your sacrifice to God; receive the change in your soul and then you will see a change in your circumstances. Look for the favor of God that gives you what you have requested of Him.

God's favor on Hannah did not come immediately; it came in the process of time. But God favored her and reversed the barrenness within her. She conceived and brought forth a son named Samuel. Notice the favor of God on Hannah. He didn't give her a son, but He opened her womb so that she might receive a son through the natural order. God works from the inside to the outside. God changed her within and then He changed her without.

So instead of crying about the Peninnah in your life, go ahead and rejoice for the Peninnah in your life. Her provoking you drove you to God in desperate prayer. When God heard your prayer and your vow, He gave you favor. Praise God for your Peninnah! There is a purpose in your warfare. There is a divine reason why there are persecutors in your life. There is a divine assignment on some of the people who provoke you.

Hannah returned years later with her son in her arms, the result of her vow. And she presented him as a living sacrifice to God and she worshipped God. This daughter of Leah stood before God and gave Him praise. Praise is the greatest response to God's favor.

And Hannah's story only got better. Eli spoke a priestly blessing over Hannah and she had five more children. Hannah, which means grace, had five more children and the number five is the number of grace. God's favor gave grace to Grace! Favor and grace are linked; favor is God's reaction to the actions of humans. Grace is God's response because it pleases Him. Favor is temporary, but grace is forever. Favor is conditional, but grace is unconditional. Favor opened the door to Hannah's grace. Samuel is God's favor on Hannah, and the other five children are God's grace to Hannah. God gave Hannah a son because she made a vow, then later God said, "I'm going to do more in your life than you asked for." Hannah only asked for a son and God gave her the son. Then God looked beyond her prayer and gave her more than she asked for! God will do that for you. Pray this blessing over yourself:

God of grace, Father who loves me. You have heard my petitions. You have heard my promises made by faith. Father, You have given me favor because You have seen the pain in my soul. Father, I thank You for favor. I thank You for giving me my Samuel, the thing that I have asked for from You and the thing that I have promised to give back to You. Now Father, according to Your word, let Your grace be poured out on me. Shower me with more of Your grace and with more than I can ask or think. Father, give me grace, so I may live in grace. Bring forth Your specific purposes in my life as a testimony of Your grace. I recognize where Your favor is for a season, Your grace is a continual habitation in my life. Amen to You who gives grace, my heavenly Father.

Questions for Discussion

1. Have you encountered harassment from a person like Peninnah? How did you handle it?

2. Have you ever stopped serving God because your wait was too long?

3. What is bitterness? Have you ever been bitter?

4. Have you ever served God and your emotion wasn't in it?

5. The author had to wait nine years to see God's promise come to pass. How did long did you have to wait for God's promise to manifest in your life?

Chapter Five

Favor After the Storm

Job 1–2, 42

The servant came running to his master Job and said, "The oxen were plowing and the donkeys feeding beside them, when the Sabeans raided them and took them away—indeed they have killed the servants... and I alone have escaped to tell you."

While he was still speaking, another also came and said, "The fire of God fell from heaven and burned up the sheep and the servants, and consumed them; and I alone have escaped to tell you!"

While he was still speaking, another also came and said, "The Chaldeans formed three bands, raided the camels and took them away, yes, and killed the servants...and I alone have escaped to tell you!" (Job 1:14–17, NKJV).

When Job thought it couldn't get any worse, he saw another servant running toward him,

"Your sons and daughters were eating and drinking

wine in their oldest brother's house, and suddenly a great wind came from across the wilderness and struck the four corners of the house, and it fell on the young people, and they are dead; and I alone have escaped to tell you!" (Job 1:18–19, NKJV)

In a matter of moments Job was given the news that all his possessions were gone. Most of his servants and all of his children were dead.

Who is this man named Job and why did this happen to him?

Job was called the greatest of all men in the East. He was righteous before God. He loved God and loved his family and was blessed beyond measure until that awful day when he became a grieving father and a man who lost all his wealth. He was a victim of terrorism, and his enemy was not named Osama Bin Laden or al Qaeda. The terrorist that attacked him was the original terrorist who had intentionally declared war on the human race from the very beginning of mankind's existence. His name is Lucifer.

And when it looked like it couldn't get any worse for Job, it did. His body was attacked with painful boils, and his wife said, "Why do you still trust God and believe Him. Curse God and die!"

Job had no wealth, no servants, and no children. Now he had no health and his wife advised him to do the unthinkable—renounce God and commit suicide.

As Job struggled with loss, pain, and depression, his three best friends came to see him. For one week they were the best of friends. They came, sat down with Job, and cried with him. For seven days they felt what he felt. They were silent because they understood that what Job needed was not conversation but the presence of friends. Their silence ministered greatly to Job.

When you are going through trouble and you feel emotional pain and you are suffering from the grief of your losses, there is nothing like having good friends to sit with you and show you empathy. In the seasons of darkness and mourning, good friends are tremendous blessings.

But all too soon those good friends of Job failed him and added to his anguish. Their problem with Job was they couldn't handle Job revealing his emotions. They couldn't deal with Job being angry. They listened to Job curse the day of his birth, but they didn't really hear his cry. His friends did not understand Job was looking for rest, "Then I would have been at rest…" (Job 3:13, NKJV). "I have no rest, for trouble comes" (3:26, NKJV). Yes, he cursed the day of his birth and wished at that moment he had never been born, but that was not the cry of his heart. He was a man who wanted to rest. He was troubled in his spirit and so he cursed his birthday. And because his friends did not understand his cry, they increased his sorrow.

Eliphaz said to Job, "Those who plow iniquity and sow trouble reap the same" (4:8, NKJV). In other words, Eliphaz was saying, "Job you brought this on yourself." Have you ever been condemned like that? Have you ever said something like that to someone else? Have these words ever left your mouth? "You're just getting what you deserve."

When My Friend Showed Up

I was in the hospital, being tested. For months I had experienced dizzy spells and I was sleeping for long hours during the day, which was very unusual for me. I knew I was depressed, but I didn't know how serious my depression was. It all came to a head one

Friday in March, while I was at home. I fainted.

My wife, Vantoria, was out with our son, Bernard Quincy. When she arrived home, I had regained consciousness, but I was sweating profusely. Vantoria took me to the nearest hospital. At the hospital, I was hooked up to a monitor to measure my heart rate. The doctor who spoke to me said my heart was beating very slowly. I was admitted for tests and observation. It was the latest experience in a horrible season of my life and I wondered if things would get worse – even as I prayed for things to get better.

A friend called me that weekend and he said, "Why are you letting those people do that to you?"

I appreciated his call; he was the only friend to call me, but his words wounded me, and I started to defend myself. I replied angrily. "Why don't you tell me how I am not to let them get to me?" He had no answer.

I lay in that hospital bed wondering what I had done to deserve this. And I wondered how it all would end. Two months earlier I had contemplated resigning. I shared my thoughts with a mentor who emphatically told me leaving was not the will of God. In the hospital room, I wondered if this was the will of God. Was I supposed to stay in a situation injuring me until I was dead?

I couldn't see it then, but now I look back over that season and I rejoice because, like Job, I experienced favor after the storm.

Job went through a storm but the favor of God brought restoration to his life. He didn't get back what the devil stole; he got more.

If Job's experience does anything for you, it should cause you to see how suffering that is the result of your enemy's plot against you is a gateway to the favor of God.

Favor is on the other side of your storm. It is on

the other side of you being mistreated and attacked. Whether it's from someone in your life, or your spiritual enemy, the devil; the one that rose up against Job. Even in the hour of your despair and depression, find hope in the midst of your trouble. Because God is going to release His favor in your life and you are going to experience something phenomenal because of what you're going through. Praise God for what is going to happen in your life because of what is happening in your life!

In the first chapter of Job, we see Job's wealth and family. We see Job a righteous man, but the majority of his story deals with his sufferings, and his friends' misunderstanding of what he's going through. By the end of the book we see Job's restoration. But the lessons for us from this great man who lived in the East thousands of years ago is how to make it in the in between. How do you make it when you are in the middle of the worst? That's the answer we need to find as we glean from these months in Job's life. If you are in the season of in between, study and meditate on Job's words as you wait for the manifestation of your heavenly Father's favor.

The day God released favor on Job is recorded in Job 42:10 "And the LORD restored Job's losses when he prayed for his friends" (NKJV).

Do you know who hurt you?

Do you know who attacked you, causing you pain?

Do you know who lied about you?

Do you know who betrayed you?

Do you know what friend became your enemy?

Although it is true that we wrestle not against flesh and blood but against the devil and his kingdom, we still need to know who the devil uses against us. Not to get revenge against them, but to know for whom you need to pray. And when you pray for them, you are praying for your freedom. As you pray for them, you are preparing your heart to forgive them. Receive this principle from the life of Job: Intercession makes room in your life for restoration. Pray for the one who hurt you and caused you trouble. Pray for that person the devil used against you. Take them to the throne of God, and ask God to give mercy to them.

I Prayed for Them

I prayed for several people who did me much harm in that season. It was their actions against me that was the tool of the devil, and I knew that as I prayed for them. I prayed God would give me the grace to forgive them. As I was praying, the Spirit led me to pray for their good and to pray for prosperity in their lives. I prayed every day for 16 months for those persons. It didn't take me 16 months to forgive them. I forgave them the first time I prayed for them. It took me sixteen months to get free from the pain they caused me by their actions. And I'll never forget the day that I felt healing and freedom in my spirit. I left my desk at work and went to another building where I could have an uninterrupted period of praising and worshipping God for the breakthrough I felt in my spirit. To this day, I don't know what God did in their lives because of my intercession, but I know what He did in my life. In that season, God's favor surrounded me and I had peace. I had His presence, and I had daily bread.

Restoration occurred in my soul years before it occurred in my circumstances. Today, I'm in a greater place because I received favor after the storm.

Questions for Discussion

1. Have you ever had a day where you were told of bad

news several times? How did you respond to it?

2. Can you relate to Job's story? What great losses have you experienced in your life?

3. Have you ever been accused of bringing trouble on yourself? Have you ever accused a person of bringing trouble on you? Have you ever rejoiced at the news of someone's trouble?

4. Do you pray for persons who have hurt you?

5. Where does restoration begin?

Chapter Six

Finding Favor In Hostile Territory

Genesis 26

It's getting bad around here. The crops are dying and there is no water for the cattle. I remember my father talking about a time like this. He went to Egypt until it was over. I think I need to do the same thing.

I imagine that's what Isaac thought as he packed up his family and all of their belongings and set out for Egypt. On his way the Lord said to him, "Do not go down to Egypt; live in the land of which I shall tell you" (Genesis 26:3, NKJV). God directed Isaac to a place called Gerar.

So Isaac lived in Gerar, and there Isaac encountered his first enemy.

Before Isaac experienced enemies, life was pretty good for him. He established a place for his family to live and he started making a living by planting crops. In his first harvest, Isaac experienced the supernatural abundance of God in his life. From his crops Isaac received a hundredfold harvest, the first time in the Word of God where we see such an occurrence. After his harvest, the Word says that God blessed him.

I don't know about you, but I would have been ecstatic over a hundred percent return on my investment in the same year. Can you imagine investing one thousand dollars in your business, and in twelve months receiving a return of one hundred thousand dollars? I would be blessing God for the harvest my seeds had sown. But then after I had received a hundredfold harvest, I then discover I have been blessed after the harvest. Talk about a new level of excitement!

Isaac was blessed and his enterprise was blessed. In the land of Gerar, where Isaac had no intentions of living, God blessed him. Is that your story? Are you doing well in a town where you had no intention of living? Has God blessed you with a position in a company you had no intention of taking a position in? Has God blessed you in a church where you had no intention of going? Has God blessed you in a marriage after you decided not to get the divorce?

As exciting as Genesis 26:12 is, wait until you read verse 13. "The man began to prosper, and continued prospering until he became very prosperous" (Genesis 26:13, NKJV). It says that Isaac began to prosper. Wait! I thought he was already prosperous. I mean he gets a hundredfold return on his seed in the same year and God blesses him. But in all that he has experienced and received, God still has more for him. His harvest did not prosper him; Isaac was following the law of sowing and reaping. When you follow the law you will receive the benefits of that law, which is reaping. Isaac's prosperity was released from the blessing of the Lord.

There are many persons who reap a harvest from their seed. It has nothing to do with their relationship to God. Many don't even believe in God, but still they receive a return on their investment. This law works, whether you love God or not. This law works, whether you are saved or not. This law works, whether you are in church or not. It is a law that has been set in the universe. Just because a person is reaping from his seed does not mean he is blessed. Isaac planted seed in the ground and the harvest came forth, because he was obeying the law of sowing and reaping.

However, to be blessed by God is different. God doesn't bless everybody. God blessed Isaac because there was a covenant between them. God said to Isaac's father Abraham, "I will bless you." God said the same thing to Isaac: "If you live here, I will bless you." The blessings of God come on those who are in covenant with God and those who are obedient to God. And from that blessed state, that blessed place where Isaac lived with God in covenant relationship, Isaac began to prosper.

When he was getting all of that other stuff, he wasn't even prospering yet. It was not until the Lord laid His hands on Isaac that the son of Abraham began to prosper. And his prosperity continued until he became very prosperous. He began to prosper, he continued to prosper, and he became prosperous.

Don't be content with your paycheck—that's just your harvest from your seed. Don't be content with your investments for your retirement—that's just your harvest from your seed. Don't be content with your tax return—that's just the result of you sowing into the government, which you really didn't have a choice about. Get in the place of covenant and obedience, so God can bless you. The blessing will release your prosperity.

Psalm 25:12–13 says, "Who is the man who fears the LORD? Him shall He teach in the way He chooses.

He himself shall dwell in prosperity, and his descendants shall inherit the earth" (NKJV).

Isaac's prosperity brought enemies into his life. His enemies declared war on him. The blessings of God and your prosperity will make your neighbor your enemy.

The Philistines envied Isaac. The Philistines are a type of the world. The world doesn't mind you praising God when you are broke, but the world will despise you when you praise God and you are prosperous. The world doesn't mind the people of God going to broken down churches in broken down cars, worshipping God on broken down pews. But let a church build a magnificent edifice to the glory of God and they will attempt to stop the work of the kingdom with their complaints about the church bringing too much traffic into the neighborhood.

The Philistines' Lives

In the city where I was born and raised, there was an issue in one of the suburban localities. A concerted effort was organized by a group of citizens to stop a church from building a worship center and houses for members of their congregation. And when the mayor of that suburb supported the church, he was recalled from office.

Yes, the modern day Philistines envy the prosperity of God's people. But a greater tragedy is when God's people envy prosperity in God's people. A greater tragedy with greater consequences is when the children of God will take on the spirit of the Philistines and hate a prosperous brother or sister. So many of God's children have to hide their prosperity because the members of the churches where they attend are envious and despise those who are blessed. Many pastors whom God has blessed have been the object of scorn and jealousy in the church.

The Philistines in the Church

A couple in this church that I pastored received a very large financial settlement, and they purposed to give their tithes off the settlement. The couple also wanted to give half toward the purchase of a car for me if the church would give the other half. The couple was discouraged from blessing me by the hostility shown by some other members. One of the more "spiritual" members told them it wasn't God's will for them to bless me in that manner. There was such a spirit of envy in that church against this couple.

Another time I was in the company of a group of these Philistines and they were saying terrible things about a pastor and his congregation because he lived in a mansion. They accused the members of his church of being in a cult and even told lies that the members had to bring their paychecks to the pastor so the pastor would know what his members made. There is a spirit of the Philistines in God's house and we must be freed from it. We need to stop despising the blessings of others. We should start celebrating the goodness of God when we see it manifesting in a believer's life!

The Philistines could not stop Isaac's prosperity, so they tried to hurt him in another area. They stopped up his wells with dirt.

Wells were important because they provided water for crops, cattle, and family. Those wells were the means of Isaac sustaining his life and his family's life. They were not only trying to stop his blessings, but they were after his life, because without those wells, Isaac and his family would eventually die.

Envy will cause your enemy to go after your life. Cain killed Abel because of envy. Israel's sons conspired to kill their brother Joseph because they envied him. The Philistines in your life know that if they stop your blessings, you will get another one. If they stop your harvest, you can plant again and get another harvest. But if they take your life, it's all over.

In the land of his enemies, Isaac did not give up. He overcame the hand of his enemies by undoing what they had done. Like the many survivors of hurricane Katrina who returned to New Orleans, Isaac went back to the wells his father established and dug them again. A blessed and a prosperous man will never be defeated by his enemies. He will always reclaim what is his and make it equitable for himself.

Not only did Isaac reclaim his inheritance, but he also enlarged his territory by digging other wells. While he was enlarging his territory he was engaged in war. His prosperity got him put out of one place and his enlargement created opposition for him in another place. He moved away from the enemies that stopped up his wells and moved into the valley. In the valley, he met another group of enemies. This group did not try to do what the others did. They didn't want to stop up the wells; they wanted the wells for themselves. The men in the valley were thieves.

Twice Isaac had wells stolen from him. He kept moving and he kept digging wells, until he came to a place he called Rehoboth. In Rehoboth, Isaac got a revelation of God's intent. He moved one more time and came to Beersheba. There God appeared to him and confirmed their covenant.

The favor of God kept Isaac while he lived in enemy territory. God gave him favor on top of everything else because of the envy and the actions of his enemies. Isaac was blessed and Isaac was prosperous and Isaac saw the harvest of his sowing, but he didn't get favor until the Philistines rose up against him.

What is favor for a man that has so much? Favor is God moving you through hostile territory to get you to the place of peace, where you can enjoy rest from your enemies.

Favor is God using the hostility of the Philistines to get you to Beersheba. Without hostility, Isaac would have stayed in the country of the Philistines. God gave him favor when his enemies declared war on him.

When your enemies, both spiritual and natural, are waging war against you, God is moving you from one place to another. When I was a little boy growing up in church, the saints would say God is moving us from one degree of grace to another. God moved Isaac from Gerar. Although Isaac was blessed in Gerar, he was in hostile territory. But when he got to Rehoboth, he looked back and saw the favor of God and knew that God was moving him to Beersheba.

When you are moving in the midst of hostility, and when you are moving in the season of war, you can walk away from what was yours even though you know that your enemy stole it from you. Because you know you have enough within you to gain what you lost. You know your move is the favor of God. God is moving you to another place where your enemies can't get to you.

When Isaac got to Beersheba, God revealed Himself and Isaac built an altar—a place of worship where he prayed. See, you can't worship and pray living with the Philistines. When Isaac was done worshipping, he dug a well. This time, the well was his and there were no Philistines to stop it up or steal it. As he worshipped God at the altar, his enemies came to him to seek a covenant with him. Isaac didn't find peace until he left them; now his enemies were seeking peace with him. The favor of God will cause your enemies to seek peace from you.

You may believe you have enough, that you have been blessed enough, but the hands of your enemies against you will cause the favor of God to put you in a place where you will receive even more. Isaac lost two wells in Gerar. In Beersheba he received two wells!

Questions for Discussion

1. Do you believe it is God's will for you to be where you are right now?

2. Do you practice the law of sowing and reaping?

3. Have you ever been in a situation you didn't want to be in and God blessed you because of your obedience?

4. According to Psalm 25:12–13, what are the benefits of fearing God?

5. Are there any Philistines in your life?

Chapter Seven

Favor In the Lion's Den

Daniel 6

In Babylon there was a king named Darius. His government had 120 administrators, called satraps. These men were officers in Darius' court. Each satrap had civil and military jurisdiction over the province they were assigned to rule. These 120 men carried the rank of prince in Darius' kingdom. Over the 120 satraps were three governors—in the United States, they would be called presidents. Among these governors was a man named Daniel. Daniel was one of the refugees living in Babylon. His original home was Israel. Because of his gifts and abilities, he became very successful in the land of his slavery and received many promotions from the kings of that land. Daniel is now one of the three governors. The responsibility of the governors was to oversee the financial activities of the 120 satraps. The governors were responsible for keeping the satraps accountable and honest.

The Word of God said Daniel had an excellent spirit.

In other words, Daniel was a magnificent man! He was a great man. Daniel possessed a superior spirit. He was the best among the best in Darius' kingdom. His work ethics were excellent.

The foundation of his greatness resided in his spirit. A man's spirit is the deeper, immaterial, invisible part of himself that determines his character. Because Daniel had a different spirit, it made him a different man. He was not a man of pretense. He wasn't simply wearing a public face. What others observed in Daniel's life was the real thing.

There are people who desire favor and promotion, but they don't have an excellent spirit. So they wear a mask to impress people. They have a public side and a personal side and the two don't look the same. As long as they walk in this manner, they will never be who God is calling them to be. Your spirit determines your journey and where you are going. A person with a double-minded spirit will never be able to proceed to excellence and experience favor.

Many of God's people are presenting themselves as having God's favor because they want people to think they are prosperous. But until you become prosperous in your spirit, you will not prosper in your life.

Disappointed by Appearances

A few years ago I purchased a book on a subject I found very interesting. A well-known pastor wrote the book. I read that book over and again. I studied it and learned the principles from it. I made diligent efforts to apply the principles of that book in my life. I believed the author was an authority by virtue of living the same principles I was learning.

A few years later, I was saddened when I discovered the person who wrote the book wasn't using the principles himself. I was dismayed and felt cheated when this particular author's financial affairs were disclosed in public. It revealed he was living in contradiction to his writings. This man, who had failed to live the principles I had learned and applied to my life, had taught me about being prosperous in my spirit; but he was not prosperous in his spirit. He could write it, but he couldn't live it. That's true of many in the church. We can preach it, but we can't live it. We can sing it, but we can't live it. We can say it, but we can't live it.

Upon hearing the news of this pastor, I shared my disappointment with an associate who called me naïve. He said, "Man, don't you know that most writers don't believe the stuff that they write? And more than that, they don't live it."

I agreed with him. And have since learned many experts are not experts because of their example, but because of their ability to successfully articulate a matter.

But Daniel was consistent because of what was in his spirit. What was on the inside of Daniel was apparent on the outside.

Having an excellent spirit put Daniel on the path to promotion. The Bible says King Darius was thinking about setting Daniel over the entire kingdom. This was astounding, considering that Daniel was a political refugee living and working in a land he was not born in. He was a son of Israel, brought to Babylon as a slave. He had risen to be one of the three governors and was being considered by the king to become the head over the two who served with him as co-governors. Daniel was on his way; promotion was within his reach.

I challenge you to be like Daniel. If you are like Daniel, the time is coming because of the excellent spirit in you. Those who walked with you will walk behind you.

Those who were your friends will be left behind as you go forward in the destiny that God has called you to.

Members of your family, whom you love and grew up with, will not be able to go where you are going. It will not be because you are better than them, but because you have excellent spirit and excellence cannot walk with mediocrity.

I believe God is placing His people strategically in places where they are about to be promoted. God has positioned you for influence; God is moving you away from mediocre people and mediocre positions.

Because Daniel had an excellent spirit in him, it caused a negative reaction in the men who were around him. The king's thoughts about promoting Daniel became public and Daniel's co-governors and the satraps conspired against him. They looked for anything that would discredit Daniel, but they couldn't find anything. And then finally they did find something—they found out he was faithful. He was faithful to God and he was faithful to Darius. And that was where they found an opportunity to get Daniel out of the picture.

It was clear to everyone in the kingdom to whom Daniel was faithful, because he didn't hide his loyalty.

The other governors and the satraps persuaded the king to enact a law that stated he would be worshipped as a god for 30 days. When Daniel heard about the law, he made a decision to do what he always did: he went home and prayed to his God. His relationship with God was the cause of his prosperity and potential promotion. Now it would become the cause of his persecution.

Daniel's enemies went to Darius to accuse Daniel. In Daniel 6:13, they called Daniel a captive and not a governor. Their words revealed what they thought of

Daniel. Your enemies will always reject the excellence in you by speaking about your past identity. They will not acknowledge who you are today.

Your enemies will constantly magnify what you were and minimize who you are today.

Darius wanted to rescue Daniel from his own law, but he could not. Darius wanted to give favor to Daniel, but he was bound by the law.

Darius may be your supervisor, he may be your husband, or she may be your wife. He may be a good friend, but there are some things Darius can't do for you. The favor of man can't rescue you from your enemies all the time. You may be prolonging your time in a situation because you are looking for Darius to rescue you and he can't.

Darius couldn't deliver his valued servant, so Daniel was thrown in the lion's pit. His enemies rejoiced because they knew they had gotten rid of Daniel.

Daniel looked to God to deliver him and God poured out His favor on Daniel. God didn't deliver Daniel from the lions' den, but He kept Daniel from the lions.

When Darius came to the den the next morning, he asked Daniel, "Has your God...been able to deliver you?" (Daniel 6:20, NKJV).

Daniel answered, and Darius knew that Daniel's God was real. The favor of God on Daniel delivered Daniel, vindicated Daniel, and prospered Daniel. God's favor will do the same thing for you. When your enemies set you up, God will give you favor in the lion's den and bring you out.

Questions for Discussion

1. Do you have an excellent spirit? What are the characteristics of an excellent spirit?

2. If a person writes about a subject, but doesn't live it, is he/she an authority?

3. Have you ever been in a position where you had to compromise your beliefs because of your position? What did you do?

4. Do you know the difference between human favor and divine favor?

5. Do your coworkers and family know to whom you are loyal?

Chapter Eight

Favor In the Furnace

Daniel 3

It was a depressing day for me, and I had been having a lot of those. But this day was different because I was venting to God. I was complaining. I was hurting. I was asking God why things had happened to me like they did. Why had I gone through what I had gone through? I wanted answers to my questions.

I asked God about every negative experience I had encountered in the last three years. I asked Him about the time we had seen a great breakthrough manifest in the church during the annual revival, only to have it defeated by carnality and the divisive actions of members in a meeting a few days later.

I asked Him about the satanic attack on me and my family while we were out of town and the terrible season we encountered from that attack.

I asked Him about the time the transmission in my car died and I didn't have $2,300 to have it repaired, so

I ended up having to return the car to the finance company to whom I still owed two years of car payments.

I asked Him about our move from the ministry we had been in for five years and the terrible encounters and spiritual warfare we faced in the new ministry.

I asked Him about the depression I suffered from, and that day in March when I fainted and my wife had to take me to the hospital where I discovered I was suffering from a hormonal imbalance and was clinically depressed.

I asked Him about the friends that had forsaken me. I recounted that the only friend who called me during that time had called to criticize me about how I had let those people get to me.

I asked Him if I did the right thing by quitting and returning home to Ohio.

I asked Him about my failures and I asked him if I was a failure. I wanted to know what I could have learned from what I was going through. As I poured out my heart to God, as I poured out my pain and disappointments to God, as I sat in His presence and complained about my past, God spoke to me. His word to me altered my life and gave me a great peace to make it through that season to new seasons that were coming. I heard the Spirit say to me as I read in the book of Daniel chapter 3,

I took you through those times as I took the three through the furnace. All of this has been to purify you. I am using your pain and rejection and betrayal and isolation to burn out of you everything that is traditional and religious. I am burning off of you everything that has held you back. When you come out of this season, you will not be the same. As I was with them in the furnace, I am with you in the furnace. You will never be alone, and when you come out of the furnace, all will witness the purifying you went through.

I want you to know today as I discovered that day: there is favor in the furnace! Shadrach, Meshach, and Abednego faced the anger of the king because they would not worship his false god. These three men of God would not join the religion of their environment. They would not serve the gods of Nebuchadnezzar.

They were faced with a choice to worship Nebuchadnezzar's god or remain true to their God, who was the one true and living God.

I am convinced that Shadrach, Meshach, and Abednego went through this experience because God ordained that He would reveal Himself to the rest of us who would go to the furnace because of persecution.

There is an appointment with your fiery furnace. There is someone in your life who is saying, "Who is the God who will deliver you?" And they will see your God when He keeps you in the furnace and when He brings you out of the furnace.

The three put their God against the god of the king. When they spoke, when they took a stand, the Word says the king's face changed toward them. Nebuchadnezzar did not know how important God was to them until they took a stand. When they did that, his face changed toward them. He had placed them in their positions. He had made them great in his kingdom. And now they rewarded his favor by rejecting his god. He no longer felt the same way about them. His face changed toward them, because his heart changed toward them. His affections turned to hatred and he commanded they be destroyed in a furnace seven times hotter than usual.

The king turned up the heat seven times hotter. There is a prophetic pattern given here. Seven is the number of perfection and completion. What Nebuchadnezzar used in an attempt to destroy the three servants of God, God used to perfect them and complete their testimony before the heathen king.

There Was an Assignment to My Furnace

Many times while I was in the furnace, I knew the
enemy of my soul was trying to destroy me. He was
trying to destroy my family. He was trying to destroy
my marriage. He was trying to destroy the future God
had for me. There were days when I didn't know how
I was going to stand under the pressure and the pain,
but what was ordered by the devil for my destruction,
God used for my perfection.

Nebuchadnezzar threw them into the furnace,
bound. They were bound in their clothing.

I was thrown into the furnace, bound. I was bound
by religion and traditions and experiences that had
no biblical value. I had been shaped from boundaries
that existed from growing up black and poor. I had
been bound by growing up in the ghetto and seeing
and experiencing things a child should not see and
experience. I was bound by my history. I was bound by
negative experiences I had growing up in the church. I
was bound by the experiences that wounded me in the
pastorates I had served. In that season of my life, God
let the enemy throw me in the furnace to burn every
form of bondage that limited my perspective.

When Shadrach, Meshach, and Abednego were
thrown into the furnace bound, they fell down.

Like them I fell down. I fell in my spirit. I fell in
my emotions. I fell down under the weight of everything I had been through. I was broken and the place
I was headed was down. And in that place God did
something in me and for me. God showed me FAVOR.
Favor was the heat that He used to loose me! He used
the heat of that furnace to set me free! He used demonic persecution and human isolation to burn off of

me everything that had me bound. I found freedom in the furnace because the heat burned off my clothing of bondage.

And the devil looked in expecting to see me dead in the furnace. Not physically dead—he thought that I would curse my God. He thought I would curse my destiny. He thought I would curse my family. He thought I would curse the church. But when he looked in, the devil saw me not dead, but alive. He saw me not bound, but loosed. He saw me not paralyzed, but walking. And he saw me not alone, but in the presence of my Lord who had promised me He would never leave me nor forsake me.

In that season, the Holy Spirit said this to me:

Your time in the furnace is not an event. It will not be like you going to church and getting what you need in a service. It will be for a season, and in that season I am walking with you in the furnace. As long as you are there I will be there with you.

And in the furnace:

I received a supernatural prayer language,

I received a new anointing in ministry,

I saw mountains fall,

God provided for me and my family in the wilderness, and

I started writing my first novel, which was released in 2009.

At the beginning of a new year I heard the Spirit say, Come out, it's over. I knew in my spirit the season was over. What I had gone through was over. It was over.

On the night before, at a New Year eve's service, I preached this Word from Deuteronomy 34—Bury your past, mourn, and move on. That word blessed me. My home church and I celebrated as we moved into a new year. But for me it was a benediction to all I had gone through. I had buried the past, I had buried the bond-ages, I had mourned what I had lost, and I was moving on. I was free. I was outside of the furnace.

Questions for Discussion

1. Have you ever examined your life and considered yourself a failure?

2. God has a purpose for your furnace and the enemy has a purpose for your furnace: do you know the difference?

3. What testimony did you receive from your furnace experience?

4. What bondage do you have in your life?

5. What did you gain from your season in the furnace?

Conclusion

In the Presence of my Enemies

At the beginning of this writing, I shared a familiar verse with you from the 23rd Psalm. Verse 5 says, "You prepare a table before me in the presence of my enemies; You anoint my head with oil; my cup runs over" (NKJV). From this verse, the Holy Spirit gave me this revelation a few years ago that I want to leave with you. You are a sheep in the fold of the Lord and He is your shepherd. Because of your relationship with the Lord, there are enemies that seek to separate you from the Shepherd and destroy you. As you follow the Shepherd, He always discerns the presence of your enemies, even when you are not aware they are near. When your enemies surround you, the Lord leads you to a table. Another word for table is mesa, which is an elevated area with steep sides. God your Shepherd leads you to a high place where your enemies can't get to you.

On the table are blessings the Shepherd has made just for you. On the table are opportunities specially designed just for you. And the Shepherd makes this table in the presence of your enemies. While your enemies have been hurt by drought, and by recessions, the Shepherd has provided a table for you in their presence.

Not only has the Shepherd provided things for you, but the Shepherd also has people for you. On the table are relationships the Shepherd has revealed to you in the presence of your enemies. There were times when it seemed that all you were surrounded by were enemies. It seemed like all the people in your life were negative and unproductive and against you, but when the Shepherd moved you it brought you to people who provided encouragement and friendship.

At the table, the Shepherd provides you with a word that will help you in the presence of your enemies. He will give you a word that causes you to rest.

The Shepherd will provide you relief from the taunts and accusations of your enemies.

At the table is your peace. You will see your enemies and not even fear them.

The table is not only a place of provision, but it is a place of vision. The Shepherd will cause you to look at your enemies in a new light. They will no longer intimidate you. The sight of them will no longer bother you. You will see them differently. And you will rejoice. You will understand that because they are present in your life, they are the cause of your table. It is because of them that you are in this place! You are at the table because of their presence in your life! You have favor because of your enemies. You ought to give God praise! He used your enemies to do so much in your life. And God will continue to do much more in your life because of your enemies.

You are a candidate for favor because of the actions of your enemies against you. What they meant for evil, God meant for good – so he could give you Divine Favor.

About the Author

Bernard Boulton is a native of Cleveland, Ohio. He is married to Vantoria Larkins Boulton and they are the parents of Bernard Quincy Boulton. Bernard is the pastor of the New Mine Creek Church in Blairs, Va. He has authored the novel *Do You Wanna Be Made Whole?* and the

Pastor Bernard Boulton

short story Jake and Eric which appears in the anthology *Home Again.*

Bernard entered his preaching ministry at the age of seventeen and has preached throughout the United States and in Haiti and Nigeria over the last 28 years. *Divine Favor: God Acts for You When Your Enemies Act Against You* is his first non-fiction inspirational writing. He is currently writing his second novel, *The Dexter's.*

Contact Bernard Boulton online at:

His website: www.bernardboulton.com
His blog: www.bernardboulton.blogspot.com
His facebook page: www.facebook.com/pabernardboulton

CPSIA information can be obtained at www.ICGtesting.com
Printed in the USA
LVOW06s0420160813

348119LV00002B/123/P